Quick and Easy Family Camping Recipes: Delicious Foil Packet Meals

by Jennie Davis

This book contains material protected under International and Federal Copyright Laws and Treaties. Any unauthorized reprint or use of this material is prohibited. No part of this book may be reproduced or transmitted in any form or by any means, electronic or mechanical, including photocopying, recording, or by any information storage and retrieval system without express written permission from the author.

© 2013 All rights reserved.

Disclaimer:

While we endeavor to keep the information in this book up to date and correct, we make no representations or warranties of any kind, express or implied, about the completeness, accuracy, reliability, suitability or availability with respect to the book or the information, products, services, or related graphics contained in the book for any purpose. Any reliance you place on such information is therefore strictly at your own risk.

In no event will we be liable for any liability, loss or damage including without limitation, indirect or consequential loss or damage, or any loss or damage whatsoever arising from loss of data or profits arising out of, or in connection with, the use of the material or the interpretation of the material contained in this book.

Dedication:

This book is dedicated to all the camp cooks out there. I hope these recipes bring you as much joy as they've brought me.

Contents

Foil Packet Cooking 9
Making a Foil Packet 10
Cooking Techniques... 12
Foil Packet Cooking Tips... 14
Breakfast 16
    Breakfast Burritos.. 17
    Cheesy Bacon Potatoes 19
    Egg in an Avocado 20
    Egg Muffin 21
    Orange Peel Eggs 23
    Sausage, Peppers and Zucchini 24
    Steak and Eggs 25
Beef and Pork Dishes 26
    Apricot Pork Chops 27
    Bacon Burgers 28
    Burger and Beans 30
    Chuck Steak Stew.. 31
    Cowboy Steak Packets 32
    Ham, Asparagus and Potatoes 33

Ham and Pineapple 34

Ham and Swiss 35

Hamburger and Veggies 36

Honey Barbecue Boneless Pork Ribs 37

Hot Dogs 38

Korean Steak 39

Lemon Thyme Steak and Asparagus 40

Potatoes and Meatballs 41

Peach Pork Chops 42

Black Beans and Sausage 43

Sirloin Steak on a Veggie Bed 44

Chicken and Turkey Dishes 45

Asparagus and Chicken 46

Broccoli Chicken 47

Cheesy Bacon Chicken 48

Chicken and Potatoes 49

Easy Italian Chicken and Veggies 50

Hawaiian Chicken 51

Jerk Seasoned Wings 52

Parmesan Chicken 54

Pepper-Stuffed Chicken Breasts 55

Quick Buffalo Wings 56

Spicy Southwest Chicken 57

Turkey-Stuffed Zucchini 58

- Seafood 60
  - Beer Shrimp 61
  - Cajun Catfish 62
  - California Clambake 63
  - Coconut Shrimp 64
  - Cod with Tomatoes and Olives 65
  - Fish Tacos 66
  - Fresh Lemon Butter Fish 67
  - Lemon Thyme Trout 68
  - Lobster Scampi 69
  - Mussels 70
  - Orange Shrimp 71
  - Chicken and Shrimp Jambalaya 72
  - Shrimp Fajitas 73
  - Shrimp Scampi 74
  - Simple Salmon 75
  - Swordfish 76
  - Teriyaki Salmon 77
  - Tilapia and Zucchini 78
- Fruit and Veggies 79
  - Apple Pie (Made in an Apple) 80
  - Balsamic Tomatoes 81
  - Blackened Yams 82
  - Creamy Cheddar Bacon Corn 83

Garlic Sage Carrots 84
Ginger Green Beans 85
Honey Peaches 86
Grilled Russet Potatoes 87
Hot Olives 88
Jalapeno Poppers 89
Loaded Baked Potato 90
Mexican Corn on the Cob 91
Minty Snap Peas 92
New Potatoes 93
Parmesan Zucchini 94
Roasted Garlic 95
Rosemary Potatoes 96
Simple Corn on the Cob 97
Simple Shrooms 98
Summer Squash and Halibut 99
Swiss Chard with Bacon 100
Stuffed Bell Peppers 101
Cherry Tomatoes and Feta 102
Desserts and Assorted Dishes 103
Banana Boats 104
Cinnamon Brown Sugar Oatmeal 105
Cheesy Salsa Dip 106
Cheesy Breadsticks 107

Chili Cheese Fries 108
Cinnamon Pineapple Doughnut Delight 109
Easy Mac and Cheese 110
Marshmallow Cinnamon Peach Halves 111
Mini Fruit Pies 112
Nachos 113
Orange Caramel Cinnamon Rolls 114
Orange Muffins 115
Quesadillas 116
Peanut Butter S'Mores Tortillas 117
Waffle Cone S'mores 118
The Best Recipe of All 119
Additional Reading 121

Foil Packet Cooking

If you're looking for quick and easy camping recipes, foil packet meals are the way to go. All you have to do with most recipes is place the ingredients onto a piece of foil, wrap them up and either toss the packet in the campfire or place it on the grill to cook.

Foil packet meals are campfire cooking broken down to the bare essentials. You can whip up entire meals in a few minutes and have dinner done in less than half an hour. Some of the meals in this book are so easy you'll have dinner done in less than 15 minutes.

The best part about foil packet cooking is there is virtually no clean-up required after the meal. The meals are cooked in the packet, so there are no dirty pots or pans to clean. You can eat the meals straight out of the foil packets, so you won't have any dishes to do. If you use regular silverware, you might have to clean off a fork or spoon. Or you can use plastic silverware, in which case you won't have anything to clean at all.

If you want to save even more time, you can prepare the foil packets ahead of time. All you'll have to do when you get back to your campsite after a long day of camping is grab a handful of foil packets and toss them in the campfire. How's that for an easy meal when all you want to do is relax by the fire?

Making a Foil Packet

Foil packets are easy to make.

Pull a section of aluminum foil off the roll. Make sure you have enough foil to wrap your food in. It's ok if you pull off too much foil, as a bit of space in your packet will create a steam pocket that will help cook your food. Allowing room for steam is preferable in many foil packet recipes as it will help the food cook faster.

Next, place your food in the center of the piece of foil and fold the ends of the foil up so the long ends of the foil are touching. Fold the two short sides of the packet in a few times, so you now have a packet that's closed off on the sides and open on the top.

Add any liquids you have to add. The short sides of the packet should be folded tightly enough so liquids will not leak out.

Once the liquids have been added (if there are any), Fold the long, open portion of the packet down a few times until you have a sealed packet that can be placed in the campfire.

I like to double up on the foil to create a sturdy packet that I don't have to worry about accidentally poking holes in. To double up the foil, just follow the folding instructions again, placing the packet you just created inside the new packet you're folding. There's nothing more frustrating than cooking a foil meal only to open it and find all the liquids have drained out and the food is a dried out mess. Heavy duty foil works best for foil packet cooking.

Remember to leave room for steam when you're folding down the top of the packet if you have raw vegetables in the packet that need to be steamed. If you want to speed up the cooking process, try substituting vegetables that have already been cooked for the raw vegetables in the recipes.

If you're cooking meats that you don't want to be steamed, fold the packet all the way down to the food. This will brown the meats more than if you leave room for steam to form. It will also char vegetables if you cook them long enough.

Cooking Techniques

There are a number of ways you can cook your foil packets. Here are the most common foil packet cooking methods:

- **In the campfire.** The packets can be placed directly in the campfire. This method will cook the food quickly, but it may cook unevenly, as there will be hotspots in the coals.
- **On a grill over the campfire.** A grill over the campfire allows you to utilize your campfire without having to place the foil packets directly in the coals. The food will cook more evenly than it will when the packets are placed in the coals. Don't cook your packets over an open flame. Instead, cook them over hot embers.
- **On a barbecue grill.** Fire up the briquettes and let them burn down to coals. Place the foil packets on the grill to cook. This technique of cooking your foil packet meals gives you the most control over temperature.
- **In the oven.** This isn't a camping technique, but you can fire up the oven and cook foil packets when you're at home when you want a quick and easy meal.

Regardless of the cooking method used, it's important to realize campfire cooking isn't an exact science. The cook times in the recipes in this book are estimates and there are a lot of variables that can cause them to be wildly inaccurate.

It's important that you monitor your food closely. Check packets regularly while cooking to see how cooked the food inside is. It's best to err on the side of caution when checking packets. If you open a packet and it isn't done yet, you can always put it back on the grill. If you wait too long and the food is burnt, there isn't much you can do to rescue it.

Foil Packet Cooking Tips

The following tips should help you get the most from your foil packet meals:

- **When cooking in the campfire, avoid placing the foil packet directly in an open flame.** Instead, place it in the coals of the fire.
- **Be careful! Foil packets are full of hot steam.** While it may be tempting to put your face right next to a packet to catch a whiff as soon as you open it, you can get badly scalded by the hot steam.
- **Don't worry about being exact.** Foil packet recipes are rather forgiving when it comes to the ingredients. I very rarely measure the ingredients I'm putting in a packet. Instead, I throw in a bit of this and a bit of that until I feel like I've got things the way I want them.
- **Double wrap your foil packets.** You don't want to lose half of your food through a hole in the bottom of your packet. You also don't want to accidentally poke a hole in your packet while eating and have hot juices run out into your lap.
- **If you want your vegetables to come out crisp and a little charred, try poking a few holes in the foil packet with a fork.** Be careful not to get ashes or hot coals in the holes you poke if you're cooking directly in the campfire.
- **If you're planning on dumping the contents of the foil packet onto a plate to eat them, cut the top off**

of the foil packet with a pair of scissors. The foil packet will be hot and trying to unfold it is an exercise in frustration. Using scissors will allow you to open the packet without burning your fingers.
- **Use boiled vegetables to speed things up.** Pre-cooked carrots, potatoes and celery will really speed up the cooking times for recipes that call for these items.
- **When you're cooking foods that don't have a lot of moisture, add a bit of butter to the inside of the foil packet to keep the food from sticking to the foil.** Cooking spray will also work.
- **You can eat your food straight out of the foil packet if you want.** Cut an X in the top of the foil packet and fold the foil back, giving you easy access to your food.
- **You can speed things up in couple of ways.** Create the spice blends ahead of time and bring them in a Ziploc baggy. Another way to speed things up is to create the foil packets in advance and bring the ready-to-go packets in the ice chest. All you'll have to do is toss the packets on the fire.

Breakfast

Breakfast is one of the most important camp meals of the day because it provides you the energy you need to make it through until lunch time, which could be late in the day, depending on what you're doing. Foil packet breakfasts are a quick and easy way to fill your stomach and set the stage for the busy day ahead.

Think of camping breakfast as fuel for the day ahead. If you don't put enough fuel in your tank, you'll run out of gas before the day is complete. Make sure you eat enough food, as most camping activities burn a lot of calories.

Breakfast Burritos

Ingredients:

3 eggs
¼ pound sausage
¼ cup onions, chopped
1 green onion, chopped
½ cup mushrooms, sliced
1 medium potato, peeled and cubed
1 cup shredded Mexican blend cheese
1 tablespoon fresh parsley, chopped
Salt and pepper, to taste

2 flour tortillas
Cilantro, for garnish
Sour cream, for topping

Directions:

1. Add the eggs to a small bowl and scramble them.
2. Add the rest of the ingredients to the foil packet and fold it up, leaving the top open.
3. Pour the eggs over the contents of the foil packet.
4. Seal foil packet tightly.
5. Cook the packet for 10 minutes. Open the packet carefully and stir the contents.
6. Cook for an additional 10 minutes, or until potatoes are soft. To speed up the cooking time, boil the potatoes beforehand.
7. Remove packet from heat and cut X in top.
8. Spoon contents into tortillas.

9. Garnish with cilantro and add sour cream, to taste.

Cheesy Bacon Potatoes

Ingredients:

10 baby red potatoes, sliced into thin coins
½ cup bacon, cooked and crumbled

2 tablespoons butter
½ cup cheddar cheese, shredded
Salt and pepper, to taste

Directions:

1. Place potatoes on foil.
2. Break butter into pieces and spread across potatoes.
3. Spread bacon over top.
4. Wrap foil packet up tightly.
5. Cook for 20 to 25 minutes, or until potatoes are cooked to your liking. If you want the potatoes browned a bit, poke a few holes in the top of the foil packet before cooking.
6. Once potatoes are cooked, remove from heat and open foil packet carefully
7. Add cheese to the packet.
8. Reseal the packet and let it sit for a few minutes to allow for the cheese to melt.
9. Open the packet, stir the contents and enjoy.

Egg in an Avocado

Ingredients:

1 avocado half
1 egg
Salt and pepper to taste

Directions:

1. Cut avocado in half and remove seed. Scoop out part of the avocado to make room for the egg.
2. Crack egg and dump contents into the avocado.
3. Wrap in foil.
4. Cook for 15 to 20 minutes, or until egg is cooked to your liking.
5. Carefully unwrap packet and season the egg with salt and pepper.

Egg Muffin

NOTE: These egg muffins can be made in advance and wrapped in foil. Cook the eggs beforehand and wrap each muffin in foil. When you're hungry, all you'll have to do is warm up the muffins for an instant breakfast snack anytime you want.

Ingredients:

1 English muffin
1 slice cheddar cheese
1 hash brown patty
1 sausage patty
1 egg

Salt and pepper, to taste

Directions:

1. Place the hash brown patty on the foil.
2. Wrap the packet around the hash brown patty. Leave the top open.
3. Crack the egg and dump the contents over the top of the hash brown patty.
4. Place the sausage patty on top of the egg.
5. Close the foil packet.
6. Cook for 10 to 15 minutes, or until egg is cooked to your liking.
7. Remove packet from heat.
8. Open packet and season with salt and pepper.

9. Place contents of packet on half an English muffin. Add cheese to the top and place the other half of the muffin on top to make a sandwich.

Orange Peel Eggs

Ingredients:

1 orange
2 eggs
Salt and pepper, to taste

Directions:

1. Cut the orange in half and scoop out the meat. Leave the peel intact. When done, you should have 2 empty orange halves.
2. Crack an egg into each of the orange halves.
3. Wrap each half in its own foil packet. Be careful to keep the orange peel upright, so the egg doesn't spill out.
4. Cook the packet for 10 to 15 minutes, or until the eggs are cooked all the way through.
5. Remove the packet from the heat.
6. Open it carefully and season the egg with salt and pepper.

Sausage, Peppers and Zucchini

Ingredients:

1 large sausage, sliced diagonally
1 zucchini, sliced diagonally
5 new potatoes, quartered
1 red bell pepper, seeded and sliced
½ medium onion, sliced

Salt and pepper, to taste

Directions:

1. Combine all ingredients in a foil packet.
2. Seal the packet up tightly.
3. Cook for 25 to 30 minutes, or until sausage is cooked and vegetables are soft.

Steak and Eggs

Ingredients:

½ pound carne asada
2 tablespoons taco seasoning
2 eggs
½ cup Mexican blend cheese

Directions:

1. Cut carne asada up and place in foil packet with taco seasoning.
2. Crack the eggs and dump them into the packet.
3. Mix the steak and eggs together.
4. Cook for 15 to 20 minutes, or until steak and eggs are cooked.
5. Open foil packet and sprinkle cheese on top.
6. Eat the steak and eggs on their own or add them to a tortilla to make a breakfast burrito.

Beef and Pork Dishes

The recipes in this section include some of my personal favorite camping dishes. When I go camping, I'm all about comfort foods. The recipes in this section are, in my opinion, some of the best comfort foods around.

I don't limit myself to cooking these recipes while camping. I've been known to fire up the grill at home and cook up a quick packet when I feel like eating something filling and delicious.

Apricot Pork Chops

Ingredients:

1 pork chop

1 cup apricot preserves
1 tablespoon butter, melted
1 teaspoon balsamic vinegar

Directions:

1. Combine butter, apricot preserves and vinegar and stir together.
2. Place pork chop on foil and coat with peach preserve mixture.
3. Wrap tightly in foil packet.
4. Cook for 15 to 20 minutes, or until pork is cooked all the way through.

Bacon Burgers

NOTE: These burgers can be made in advance and wrapped in foil. Cook the bacon burgers ahead of time and build the burgers at home. When you're hungry, all you'll have to do is warm up the burgers up until they're cooked all the way through and the cheese is melted. We usually build 15 to 20 burgers in advance, so the kids can warm one up as a snack anytime they want.

Ingredients:

1 hamburger patty
2 sliced of bacon
1 slice of cheddar cheese
Salt and pepper, to taste

Hamburger bun
Condiments

Directions:

1. Wrap bacon pieces around hamburger and pin in place with a toothpick. If you wrap the bacon around the top and place it under the hamburger, you can probably get away with not using a toothpick.
2. Place on foil and wrap foil tightly around the burger.
3. Cook for 12 to 15 minutes, or until burger is cooked to your liking.
4. Remove from heat and open carefully.

5. Place cheese on bacon burger and place burger on bun.
6. Add condiments to your liking.

Burger and Beans

Ingredients:

¼ pound hamburger
½ onion, diced
½ cup baked beans
¼ cup barbecue sauce
A handful of bread crumbs
Salt and pepper, to taste

Directions:

1. Combine the hamburger, onion, barbecue sauce and bread crumbs, salt and pepper in a bowl and mix together.
2. Form the hamburger into a patty and place the patty on the foil.
3. Pour beans over the top.
4. Seal the foil packet tightly.
5. Cook for 20 to 25 minutes, or until hamburger is cooked to your liking.

Chuck Steak Stew

Ingredients:

1 pound chuck steak, cubed
1 package onion soup mix
2 potatoes, peeled and cut into chunks
2 carrots, peeled and cut into coins
¼ cup water
½ cup mushrooms, sliced
2 tablespoons olive oil
Salt and pepper, to taste

Directions:

1. Add all ingredients to a foil packet and mix together.
2. Wrap packet up. Leave room for steam to form.
3. Cook packet for 30 to 45 minutes, or until steak is cooked all the way through and the vegetables are soft.
4. If you want a thicker stew, add a few tablespoons of flour at a time and stir it in until the stew is of the desired consistency.

Cowboy Steak Packets

Ingredients:

½ pound sirloin steak, cubed
½ cup broccoli florets
1 red bell pepper, seeded and sliced
1 small onion, sliced
4 new potatoes, sliced

2 tablespoons fresh parsley
1 tablespoon garlic pepper
2 tablespoons olive oil
Salt and pepper, to taste

Directions:

1. Add all ingredients to a bowl and mix together.
2. Place contents of bowl into a foil packet and seal it tight.
3. Place in campfire and cook for 20 to 25 minutes, or until steak and veggies are cooked to your liking.

Ham, Asparagus and Potatoes

Ingredients:

1 large ham steak, cut into pieces
10 asparagus spears, broken into pieces
4 small red potatoes, cut into pieces
½ cup Alfredo sauce

Directions:

1. Combine all ingredients in a foil packet.
2. Seal the foil packet, leaving room for steam.
3. Cook for 15 to 20 minutes, or until asparagus is soft.

Ham and Pineapple

Ingredients:

1 ham steak, cut into chunks
3 pineapple rings, cut into chunks
1 sweet potato, cubed

2 tablespoons brown sugar
2 tablespoons butter

Directions:

1. Add all ingredients to foil packet.
2. Seal packet up, leaving room for steam.
3. Cook for 15 to 20 minutes, or until pineapple and potatoes are cooked.
4. Flip packet after 10 minutes.
5. Let cool for 10 minutes before opening packet.

Ham and Swiss

Ingredients:

Ham lunch meat, thinly sliced
½ loaf sourdough bread
2 tablespoons butter
5 slices of Swiss cheese

Directions:

1. Slice the loaf of sourdough bread into 10 slices and place the loaf on the foil.
2. Spread a bit of butter between every other piece.
3. Place a slice of Swiss cheese and few pieces of lunchmeat next to the same pieces of bread you spread the butter on, making 5 sandwiches.
4. Wrap the loaf of bread up tightly.
5. Cook for 15 to 20 minutes, or until the cheese is melted all the way through. Flip the foil packet after 7 minutes.

Hamburger and Veggies

Ingredients:

½ pound ground beef
½ can cream of mushroom soup
¼ cup sliced mushrooms
¼ cup carrot coins
¼ cup corn niblets

Salt and pepper, to taste

Directions:

1. Add all ingredients to a foil packet and seal the packet up.
2. Cook for 30 to 45 minutes, or until veggies are soft and hamburger is cooked.

Honey Barbecue Boneless Pork Ribs

Ingredients:

½ pound boneless pork ribs
1 cup baby carrots, halved
5 new potatoes, halved

¼ cup barbecue sauce
5 tablespoons honey
1 teaspoon cumin
½ teaspoon salt

Directions:

1. Mix the barbecue sauce, honey, cumin and salt in a small bowl.
2. Place the ribs, carrots and potatoes on the foil.
3. Pour the honey barbecue sauce over the top.
4. Wrap the foil packet, leaving a little room for steam.
5. Grill packet for 25 to 35 minutes, or until pork is cooked all the way through and potatoes are soft.

Hot Dogs

Ingredients:

2 hot dogs
½ red pepper, sliced
½ green pepper, sliced
½ onion, sliced
1 teaspoon olive oil

2 hot dog buns
Mustard, to taste

Directions:

1. Place hot dogs on foil.
2. Add peppers and onions.
3. Drizzle with olive oil.
4. Fold foil packet up tightly.
5. Cook in campfire for 15 to 20 minutes, or until hot dogs are cooked all the way through.
6. Remove from fire and open foil packet.
7. Place hot dogs, peppers and onions on hot dog buns.
8. Season with mustard, to taste.

Korean Steak

Ingredients:

½ pound steak, sliced
1 scallion, sliced thinly

2 tablespoons soy sauce
1 tablespoon rice vinegar
1 tablespoon brown sugar
1 teaspoon ginger, grated
1 teaspoon sesame oil
Red pepper, to taste

Directions:

1. Combine sauce ingredients in a bowl and stir together.
2. Place scallion and steak on foil.
3. Pour sauce over the top.
4. Fold foil packet up tightly.
5. Cook for 15 to 20 minutes, or until steak is cooked to your liking.
6. Let sit for 5 minutes before eating.

Lemon Thyme Steak and Asparagus

Ingredients:

1 sirloin steak
5 asparagus spears
1 lemon, sliced

2 teaspoons thyme
1 teaspoon butter
1 teaspoon olive oil
Salt and pepper, to taste

Directions:

1. Place steak on foil.
2. Place asparagus spears around steak.
3. Season the steak with the salt, pepper and thyme.
4. Place butter on the asparagus.
5. Drizzle olive oil over everything.
6. Place lemon slices over steak.
7. Close foil packet, leaving room for steam.
8. Cook for 12 to 15 minutes, or until steak is cooked to your liking.
9. Let sit for 5 minutes before opening foil packet.

Potatoes and Meatballs

Ingredients:

½ pound hamburger meat
½ cup carrots, chopped
5 small red potatoes, halved
½ an onion, diced

1 package dry ranch dressing
½ tablespoon salt
½ tablespoon pepper

Directions:

1. Add salt and pepper to hamburger meat and divide the meat up into meatballs.
2. Place the meatballs on the foil.
3. Add the vegetables around the meatballs.
4. Season the meatballs and vegetables with the dry ranch dressing.
5. Seal the foil packet, leaving room for steam.
6. Cook the packet for 30 to 35 minutes, or until hamburger is cooked to your liking and vegetables are soft. Flip the packet after 15 minutes.
7. Open packet carefully and enjoy.

Peach Pork Chops

Ingredients:

1 pork chop

1 cup peach preserves
1 tablespoon butter, melted
1 teaspoon balsamic vinegar

Directions:

1. Combine butter, peach preserves and vinegar and stir together.
2. Place pork chop on foil and coat with peach preserve mixture.
3. Wrap tightly in foil packet.
4. Cook for 15 to 20 minutes, or until pork is cooked all the way through.
5. Remove from heat and let the packet sit for 5 minutes before carefully opening it.

Black Beans and Sausage

Ingredients:

½ pound smoked sausage, sliced diagonally
1 can black beans, drained and rinsed
1 carrot, peeled and diced
1 shallot, diced

1 garlic clove, minced
1 cup chicken broth
Salt and pepper, to taste

Directions:

1. Combine all ingredients in a foil packet.
2. Add salt and pepper, to taste.
3. Wrap foil packet up, leaving room for steam.
4. Cook for 30 to 35 minutes, or until carrots are soft.

Sirloin Steak on a Veggie Bed

Ingredients:

1 sirloin steak
1 Russet potato, shredded
½ cup mushrooms, sliced
½ onion, chopped
½ cup green beans, halved

2 teaspoons olive oil
Salt and pepper, to taste

Directions:

1. Place shredded potato on foil.
2. Add mushrooms, onion and green beans on top of potato.
3. Drizzle 1 teaspoon of olive oil over the vegetables.
4. Rub steak with olive oil, salt and pepper.
5. Place steak on top of veggies.
6. Wrap foil packet tightly.
7. Cook for 20 to 25 minutes, or until steak is cooked to your liking and veggies are cooked all the way through.

Chicken and Turkey Dishes

The recipes in this section all use chicken in one form or another. When cooking chicken and turkey, it's important to make sure the chicken is cooked all the way through. The meat shouldn't have any pink in it and the juices should run clear when you cut into the meat.

Asparagus and Chicken

Ingredients:

2 pieces of chicken, your choice
1 cup asparagus, broken into pieces
½ cup mushrooms, sliced

½ cup cream of chicken soup

Directions:

1. Place chicken on foil packet.
2. Place asparagus and mushrooms around chicken.
3. Pour cream of chicken soup over the top.
4. Wrap foil packet up, leaving room for steam.
5. Cook for 25 to 30 minutes, or until chicken is cooked all the way through and the asparagus is soft. Flip the foil packet over after 10 minutes.

Broccoli Chicken

Ingredients:

1 chicken breast
1 cup broccoli
1 cup cooked rice

1 cup cream of mushroom soup
1 teaspoon garlic powder
½ teaspoon oregano
½ teaspoon paprika
Salt and pepper, to taste

Directions:

1. Cut chicken breast into pieces.
2. Combine all ingredients in a foil packet.
3. Wrap packet up, leaving room for steam.
4. Cook for 30 to 45 minutes, or until chicken is cooked all the way through and broccoli is soft.

Cheesy Bacon Chicken

Ingredients:

1 boneless, skinless chicken breast, cubed
6 slices bacon, cooked and broken into pieces
1 cup shredded cheddar cheese

3 tablespoons ranch dressing
2 tablespoons olive oil

Directions:

1. Coat chicken breast in olive oil and place on foil.
2. Spread ranch dressing over chicken.
3. Spread cheese over top of chicken.
4. Sprinkle bacon over top of cheese.
5. Wrap foil packet tightly.
6. Cook for 20 to 25 minutes, or until chicken is cooked all the way through.

Chicken and Potatoes

Ingredients:

1 chicken breast, cubed
1 large potato, cubed with skin left on

½ cup barbecue sauce
2 tablespoons butter
1 teaspoon seasoned salt
½ teaspoon cracked black pepper

Directions:

1. Add the potatoes to the foil packet first.
2. Place half of the butter over the potatoes.
3. Wrap the packet up and cook it for 15 to 20 minutes, or until potatoes start browning.
4. Open foil packet and add the rest of the ingredients. Mix the ingredients together as well as you can.
5. Reseal the foil packet and cook it an addition 20 to 25 minutes, or until the pieces of chicken are cooked all the way through.

Easy Italian Chicken and Veggies

Ingredients:

1 chicken breast
2 new red potatoes, sliced
10 black olives, sliced
½ cup fresh green beans, ends removed
5 cherry tomatoes

3 tablespoons Italian salad dressing

Directions:

1. Place chicken on foil.
2. Coat with Italian dressing.
3. Add vegetables around chicken.
4. Wrap foil packet up, leaving room for steam.
5. Place in campfire and cook for 25 to 30 minutes, or until chicken is cooked all the way through and vegetables are soft.

Hawaiian Chicken

Ingredients:

1 boneless, skinless chicken breast
½ cup pineapple chunks, drained
1 red pepper, sliced

½ cup teriyaki sauce

Directions:

1. Add all ingredients to foil packet.
2. Seal packet up, leaving room for steam.
3. Cook for 20 to 25 minutes, or until chicken is cooked all the way through. Flip packet over after 10 minutes.

Jerk Seasoned Wings

NOTE: The seasoning should be created at home in order to speed things up while cooking this recipe on a camping trip. Alternatively, you can buy jerk seasoning already prepared and add it to your wings.

Ingredients:

Chicken wings

2 tablespoons olive oil
¼ cup allspice
¼ cup brown sugar
3 garlic cloves
2 scotch bonnet peppers
1 tablespoon ground thyme
1 tablespoon dried minced onion
½ teaspoon cinnamon
½ teaspoon nutmeg

Directions:

1. Add all of the seasoning ingredients to a blender or food processor and blend them until thoroughly mixed.
2. Place chicken wings in a plastic bag and toss with jerk seasoning.
3. Create foil packet around wings.
4. Cook for 30 minutes. Flip the packet over after 15 minutes.

5. Make sure wings are cooked all the way through before eating.

Parmesan Chicken

Ingredients:

1 breaded chicken breast patty
4 small red potatoes, quartered
½ a small onion, diced

½ cup spaghetti sauce
3 tablespoons shredded Parmesan cheese

Directions:

1. Place chicken on foil.
2. Surround it with potatoes and onions.
3. Pour spaghetti sauce over the top.
4. Sprinkle Parmesan cheese on top.
5. Wrap foil packet up tightly.
6. Cook for 20 to 25 minute, or until chicken is cooked all the way through and potatoes are soft.

Pepper-Stuffed Chicken Breasts

Ingredients:

1 boneless chicken breast
½ cup assorted red, green and yellow peppers, sliced into strips
½ jalapeno pepper, sliced

½ teaspoon butter
1 tablespoon Dijon mustard
2 tablespoons white wine
½ teaspoon salt
½ teaspoon pepper

Directions:

1. Pound chicken breast gently until it's flattened out a bit.
2. Place peppers on chicken breast and wrap it around the peppers.
3. Pin the breast in place with a toothpick.
4. Combine butter, mustard, wine, salt and pepper in a small bowl and mix together.
5. Brush chicken breast with sauce.
6. Wrap tightly in foil packet.
7. Cook for 15 to 20 minutes, or until chicken is cooked all the way through and peppers are soft.

Quick Buffalo Wings

Ingredients:

10 chicken wings

½ cup hot sauce
½ cup barbecue sauce
½ teaspoon salt
½ teaspoon pepper

Ranch dressing

Directions:

1. Place barbecue sauce, hot sauce, salt and pepper in sealable plastic bag and mix thoroughly.
2. Place wings in bag and shake until wings are coated in sauce.
3. Place wings on foil and pour contents of bag over the top of the wings.
4. Wrap wings tightly in foil. Keep the wings in a single layer in the foil packet.
5. Cook for 25 to 30 minutes, or until wings are cooked all the way through.
6. Serve with ranch dressing.

Spicy Southwest Chicken

Ingredients:

½ pound boneless, skinless chicken breasts, cut into strips
1 green bell pepper, sliced
1 red bell pepper, sliced
½ an onion, chopped
6 olives, sliced
1 jalapeno pepper, sliced

1 teaspoon salt
A pinch of cayenne pepper

Directions:

1. Add all ingredients to foil packet and stir together.
2. Seal packet up, leaving room for steam.
3. Cook for 20 to 30 minutes, or until chicken is cooked all the way through.

Turkey-Stuffed Zucchini

Ingredients:

1 medium zucchini, halved lengthwise
¼ pound ground turkey
½ cup salsa
1 tablespoon bell pepper, diced
2 tablespoons tomato sauce

¼ teaspoon cumin
¼ teaspoon garlic powder
¼ teaspoon salt
½ teaspoon paprika
¼ teaspoon oregano

Mexican blend cheese, for topping

Directions:

1. Use a spoon or melon baller to dig a deep trench into the zucchini halves.
2. Combine the cumin, garlic powder, salt, paprika, and oregano in a small bowl.
3. Add the ground turkey, bell pepper and tomato sauce to a bowl and stir them together.
4. Combine the turkey and the spice mix and stir it together.
5. Place the zucchini halves on the foil.
6. Spoon the turkey filling into the zucchini halves. Fill them until they're overflowing.
7. Sprinkle cheese over the top.

8. Wrap the zucchini halves tightly in foil.
9. Poke a few holes in the top of the packet.
10. Cook for 25 to 30 minutes, or until the filling is cooked and the zucchini starts to soften.

Seafood

Most people are surprised to find out there are a number of tasty and easy seafood recipes that can be cooked using foil packets. From crustaceans to fish, you can enjoy a number of seafood dishes cooked in foil packets.

Remember, the cook times on these recipes are only estimates and may vary greatly depending on the heat of the coals you're cooking on. Make sure the seafood in your packets is cooked all the way through before eating it. You don't want to get sick because you ate undercooked seafood.

Beer Shrimp

Ingredients:

½ pound large shrimp, peeled and deveined
1 small shallot, sliced

1 clove garlic, chopped
½ can light beer
½ cup butter
3 tablespoons fresh lemon juice
Salt and pepper, to taste

Directions:

1. Add all of the ingredients to a foil packet and seal up tightly.
2. Cook for 35 to 45 minutes, or until shrimp are cooked all the way through.

Cajun Catfish

Ingredients:

1 catfish filet
½ can corn
½ cup red and green bell peppers, chopped
1 jalapeno pepper, chopped

1 tablespoon fresh lime juice
1 tablespoon olive oil
2 teaspoons Cajun seasoning

1 teaspoon chopped cilantro, for garnish

Directions:

1. Place catfish filet on foil.
2. Rub with 1 teaspoon Cajun seasoning.
3. Combine remaining seasoning and the rest of the ingredients and stir together.
4. Spoon over the top of the catfish.
5. Wrap foil packet up, leaving room for steam.
6. Cook for 20 to 25 minutes, or until fish is cooked all the way through.
7. Open packet and season with cilantro.

California Clambake

Ingredients:

1 pound clams
½ pound small red potatoes, sliced in half
½ pound sausage, sliced into coins

3 garlic cloves, sliced
1 cup white wine
2 tablespoons olive oil
2 tablespoons butter
½ tablespoon salt
½ tablespoon black pepper

Directions:

1. Place all of the ingredients into a foil packet.
2. Seal the foil packet. Leave room for steam.
3. Cook until clams open. This usually takes 20 to 25 minutes.

Coconut Shrimp

Ingredients:

½ pound jumbo shrimp, peeled and deveined

½ cup coconut milk
2 tablespoons lime juice
2 tablespoons shredded coconut

Directions:

1. Add all ingredients to a foil packet.
2. Fold the packet up tightly.
3. Cook for 10 to 15 minutes, or until shrimp are cooked all the way through.

Cod with Tomatoes and Olives

Ingredients:

1 cod filet
10 to 15 assorted cherry tomatoes
10 to 15 assorted olives

2 tablespoons olive oil
1 clove garlic, chopped
1 teaspoon fresh basil, chopped
1 teaspoon fresh mint, chopped
1 teaspoon oregano
½ cup chicken broth

Directions:

1. Place cod on foil.
2. Place cherry tomatoes and olives around cod.
3. Fold foil packet up, leaving room for steam. Leave the top open.
4. Add the rest of the ingredients and seal the packet.
5. Cook for 20 to 30 minutes, or until fish and tomatoes are cooked to your liking.
6. Serve hot.

Fish Tacos

Ingredients:

½ pound cod
1 lime, sliced into wedges

3 tablespoons Italian dressing
3 tablespoons cabbage, shredded
Mexican blend cheese, to taste
Sour cream, to taste
Tapatio hot sauce, to taste

1 flour tortilla

Directions:

1. Place fish on foil.
2. Coat fish with Italian dressing.
3. Squeeze limes onto fish.
4. Fold up foil packet tightly.
5. Cook for 20 to 25 minutes, or until fish is cooked all the way through.
6. Remove from heat and open foil packets.
7. Break fish into pieces and place on tortilla.
8. Add cabbage, cheese, sour cream and Tapatio, to taste.

Fresh Lemon Butter Fish

Ingredients:

1 filet of your favorite fish, preferably caught that day
½ small onion, chopped
1 lemon, halved

2 tablespoons butter
1 tablespoon fresh parsley, chopped
Salt and pepper, to taste

Directions:

1. Place fish filet on foil.
2. Add butter, onions, fresh parsley, salt and pepper to the fish.
3. Squeeze the lemon halves over the top of the fish.
4. Wrap the foil packet up tightly.
5. Cook for 15 to 25 minutes, or until fish is cooked all the way through and flaky.

Lemon Thyme Trout

Ingredients:

1 pan-size trout filet
1 lemon, sliced into wedges
1 green onion, sliced

1 sprig of thyme
2 tablespoons butter
Salt and pepper, to taste

Directions:

1. Place the fish on the foil.
2. Cut the lemon into wedges.
3. Squeeze a couple wedges onto the fish.
4. Place the remaining wedges around the fish.
5. Break butter up and place pieces of butter on top of fish.
6. Sprinkle green onions on fish.
7. Place the sprig of thyme on the fish.
8. Salt and pepper the fish, to taste.
9. Wrap the foil packet up tightly.
10. Cook for 8 to 12 minutes, or until fish is cooked all the way through.

Lobster Scampi

Ingredients:

2 lobster tails, split in half and shelled

½ cup butter
½ cup parsley, chopped
2 wedges of lemon
1 clove garlic, minced
Salt and pepper, to taste

Directions:

1. Place all ingredients in a foil packet. Squeeze the lemon wedges into the packet.
2. Seal the packet tightly.
3. Let the packet cook for 8 to 10 minute, or until lobster tails are done cooking.
4. Season with salt and pepper, to taste.

Mussels

Ingredients:

½ pound fresh mussels

½ stick unsalted butter
½ cup white wine
½ cup parsley, chopped
¼ cup lemon juice
2 cloves garlic, minced
1 tablespoon tabasco sauce

Directions:

1. Place mussels on foil packet.
2. Create a foil packet around the mussels. Leave the top open.
3. Add the rest of the ingredients to the foil packet and seal the packet up. Leave a little room for steam to form.
4. Cook until they pop open. This usually takes 10 to 15 minutes.

Orange Shrimp

Ingredients:

1 pound jumbo shrimp, peeled and deveined
3 large oranges

1 teaspoon orange zest
1 garlic clove, minced
2 teaspoons olive oil
Salt and pepper, to taste

Directions:

1. Squeeze the juice from the oranges into a sealable plastic bag.
2. Add the orange zest, garlic and olive oil to the bag.
3. Shake up the contents of the bag until the shrimp are coated.
4. Add the shrimp to the bag and shake until coated.
5. Place the shrimp onto the foil.
6. Pour the contents of the bag over the top of the shrimp.
7. Sprinkle with salt and pepper, to taste.
8. Fold the foil packet up tightly.
9. Cook for 10 to 12 minutes, or until shrimp are cooked all the way through.

Chicken and Shrimp Jambalaya

Ingredients:

¼ pound jumbo shrimp, peeled and deveined
1 boneless skinless chicken breast, boiled and cubed
1 smoked sausage, sliced diagonally
½ cup instant brown rice
½ tomato, diced
½ green bell pepper, sliced
½ red bell pepper, diced
½ cup onion, diced
1 celery stick, diced

2 teaspoons garlic powder
1 tablespoon Cajun seasoning
1 bay leaf
1 teaspoon hot sauce

Directions:

1. Combine all ingredients in a bowl and stir together.
2. Place in foil packet. You might have to divide this recipe into two foil packets.
3. Wrap foil packet up, leaving room for steam.
4. Cook for 20 to 25 minutes, or until shrimp and veggies are cooked.
5. Open packet carefully and add salt and pepper, to taste.

Shrimp Fajitas

Ingredients:

10 jumbo shrimp, peeled and deveined
½ an onion, chopped
½ a bell pepper, seeded and sliced

2 tablespoons olive oil
½ teaspoon paprika
½ teaspoon cumin
½ teaspoon cayenne pepper

Salsa, to taste
Cheese, to taste

1 tortilla

Directions:

1. Place olive oil, paprika, cumin and cayenne pepper in a sealable plastic bag and shake until mixed.
2. Place shrimp, onion and bell pepper in the bag and shake until they're coated with the seasoning.
3. Dump the contents of the bag onto a piece of foil.
4. Fold the foil packet up tightly.
5. Cook for 15 to 20 minutes, or until shrimp are cooked all the way through.
6. Place contents in a tortilla.
7. Garnish with salsa and cheese, to taste.

Shrimp Scampi

Ingredients:

½ pound shrimp, peeled and deveined

½ cup butter
½ cup parsley, chopped
2 wedges of lemon
1 clove garlic, minced
Salt and pepper, to taste

Directions:

1. Place all ingredients in a foil packet. Squeeze the lemon wedges into the packet.
2. Seal the packet tightly.
3. Let the packet cook for 8 to 10 minute, or until shrimp are done cooking.
4. Season with salt and pepper, to taste.

Simple Salmon

Ingredients:

1 salmon steak
1 lemon, sliced

2 tablespoons butter
Salt and cracked black pepper, to taste

Directions:

1. Place lemon slices on foil.
2. Lay salmon steak on top of lemon.
3. Place butter on top of salmon.
4. Add salt and cracked black pepper, to taste.
5. Fold foil packet up tightly.
6. Cook for 20 to 25 minutes, or until salmon is cooked all the way through.

Swordfish

Ingredients:

1 swordfish steak

1 large carrot, cut into strips
2 shallots, chopped
1 tablespoon butter
1 teaspoon ginger root, grated
1 teaspoon lemon juice
1 teaspoon teriyaki sauce

Directions:

1. Add all ingredients to a foil packet.
2. Fold the packet up tightly.
3. Cook for 20 to 30 minutes, or until fish and carrots are cooked.

Teriyaki Salmon

Ingredients:

1 salmon filet
½ cup teriyaki sauce
1 red bell pepper, sliced
1 green bell pepper, sliced
½ onion, sliced

Directions:

1. Place salmon on foil.
2. Arrange vegetables around salmon.
3. Pour teriyaki sauce over the top.
4. Wrap foil packet up, leaving room for steam.
5. Cook for 15 to 20 minutes, or until salmon is cooked all the way through.

Tilapia and Zucchini

Ingredients:

1 zucchini, sliced
1 tilapia filet, skinless
1 medium tomato, diced

1 tablespoon olive oil
1 tablespoon fresh basil leaves, chopped
1 clove garlic, chopped
½ teaspoon oregano
A pinch of salt
A dash of pepper

Directions:

1. Lay the zucchini slices on the foil.
2. Place the tilapia filet on top of the zucchini.
3. Place the tomato on top of the filet.
4. Sprinkle the olive oil over everything.
5. Add the garlic, oregano, salt and pepper.
6. Sprinkle the basil leaves on top.
7. Wrap the foil packet up tightly. Leave room for steam.
8. Cook for 20 minutes to a half hour, or until fish is cooked all the way through.

Fruit and Veggies

Foil packets work great for fruit and vegetable dishes. Toss in your fruit or vegetables, a bit of seasoning and fold the packet up. Place it in the fire and you'll have a tasty dish ready in as little as 10 minutes. How's that for easy and delicious?

A simple recipe that works for most veggies is a bit of salt and pepper and a teaspoon or two of olive oil. Wrap the veggies and place them in the campfire for 15 minutes to a half hour, or until the vegetables in the packet are soft. If your favorite vegetables aren't in the recipes in this section, try this recipe to see if it works.

Apple Pie (Made in an Apple)

Ingredients:

1 green apple

¼ cup apple pie filling
1 tablespoon cinnamon
1 tablespoon brown sugar
1 premade rolled pie crust

Directions:

1. Cut the top off of the apple.
2. Remove the insides to create a bowl out of the apple.
3. Mix the apple pie filling, cinnamon and brown sugar together and place it in the apple.
4. Cut a round piece out of the pie crush big enough to cover the top of the apple.
5. Place the crust over the top.
6. Cut an X into the crust.
7. Place the apple on a piece of foil and make a tight foil packet around the apple.
8. Bake for 20 to 30 minutes, or until the crust starts to brown and the apple filling is hot.

Balsamic Tomatoes

Ingredients:

2 tomatoes, cut in half

3 tablespoons, olive oil
½ teaspoon dried thyme
2 teaspoons balsamic vinegar
Salt and pepper, to taste

Directions:

1. Lay tomatoes face up on foil.
2. Drizzle olive oil over the top.
3. Add dried thyme to top of tomatoes.
4. Drizzle balsamic vinegar over tomatoes.
5. Season with salt and pepper, to taste.
6. Wrap tightly in foil.
7. Cook for 35 to 45 minutes, or until tomatoes are cooked to your liking.

Blackened Yams

Ingredients:

1 pound yams, peeled and sliced
1 green onion, sliced

2 garlic cloves, minced
1 tablespoon fresh thyme
1 sprig rosemary
4 tablespoons olive oil
Salt and pepper, to taste

Directions:

1. Place all ingredients in a foil packet and mix together.
2. Seal foil packet tightly.
3. Poke several holes in the top of the foil packet.
4. Cook foil packet for 20+ minutes, until yams are cooked to your liking.

Creamy Cheddar Bacon Corn

Ingredients:

1 ½ cups fresh corn kernels
¼ cup chopped onions
½ cup cheddar cheese, shredded
½ cup bacon, crumbled

½ cup sour cream
2 teaspoons cilantro, chopped

Directions:

1. Combine all ingredients in a foil packet and stir together.
2. Wrap packet up tightly.
3. Cook for 5 minutes.
4. Flip over and cook for 3 additional minutes.
5. Open foil packet carefully and stir contents of packet.
6. Serve warm.

Garlic Sage Carrots

Ingredients:

2 cups carrots, cut into coins

1 clove garlic, finely chopped
3 teaspoons fresh sage leaves, chopped
2 tablespoons water
1 tablespoon butter
1 teaspoon olive oil

Directions:

1. Add all ingredients except sage leaves to a foil packet and mix together.
2. Wrap foil packet up, leaving room for steam.
3. Cook for 10 to 12 minutes, or until carrots start to soften.
4. Open foil packet and sprinkle sage leaves on top.

Ginger Green Beans

Ingredients:

2 cups fresh green beans
2 cloves garlic, minced
1 teaspoon ginger root, ground

3 tablespoons soy sauce
2 tablespoons melted butter
2 tablespoons brown sugar
Salt and pepper, to taste

Directions:

1. Combine all ingredients except salt and pepper in a foil packet and mix together.
2. Seal foil packet, leaving room for steam.
3. Cook for 10 to 15 minutes, or until green beans are cooked to your liking.
4. Open packet and season with salt and pepper, to taste.

Honey Peaches

Ingredients:

1 peach, cut in half and pitted
¼ cup whipped cream

1 tablespoon coconut oil
1 tablespoon granulated sugar
½ teaspoon cinnamon
1 tablespoon honey

Directions:

1. Place peaches on foil, cut side up.
2. Drizzle coconut oil over the top of the peaches.
3. Sprinkle granulated sugar over the top.
4. Flip peaches over, so the cut side is down and wrap the foil packet up tightly.
5. Cook for 12 minutes. Flip the packet over after 6 minutes.
6. Open foil packet and flip peaches over.
7. Sprinkle cinnamon on top.
8. Drizzle with honey and fill peaches with whipped cream.

Grilled Russet Potatoes

Ingredients:

2 medium Russet potatoes, cubed
¼ onion, diced
1 clove garlic, minced

2 tablespoons parsley
2 tablespoons rosemary
1 tablespoon olive oil
1 teaspoon oregano
Salt and pepper, to taste

Directions:

1. Combine all ingredients in a bowl and stir together.
2. Place on foil and wrap up in a tight foil packet.
3. Cook for 25 to 30 minutes, or until potatoes are cooked to your liking. Turn the foil packet over every 10 minutes.

Hot Olives

Ingredients:

1 can olives

1 teaspoon red pepper flakes
2 cloves of garlic, minced

Directions:

1. Drain olives and place them on foil.
2. Wrap up packet, leaving top open.
3. Add red pepper flakes and minced garlic.
4. Toss inside packed, until mixed well.
5. Seal packet.
6. Cook for 15 minutes to a half hour, or until olives are heated all the way through.

Jalapeno Poppers

Ingredients:

5 jalapeno peppers
1 cup of your favorite cheese blend

3 tablespoons olive oil
1 teaspoon salt
½ teaspoon cumin
¼ teaspoon coriander

Directions:

1. Cut peppers in half and remove the seeds.
2. Combine olive oil, salt, cumin and coriander.
3. Rub oil blend onto the peppers.
4. Fill peppers with cheese blend.
5. Place peppers on foil and create a foil packet with room for steam.
6. Grill for 10 minutes, or until peppers are soft and cheese is melted. It's important that you keep the peppers upright while creating the packet and placing it in the campfire in order to keep the cheese inside each of the jalapeno halves.

Loaded Baked Potato

Ingredients:

1 large baking potato
2 tablespoons butter

1 cup cheddar cheese, shredded
3 tablespoons sour cream
1 green onion, chopped
3 tablespoons bacon bits

Directions:

1. Place baked potato on foil.
2. Poke holes in top of potato with a fork.
3. Coat potato with butter.
4. Wrap potato and cook until soft.
5. Open foil packet and cut potato open.
6. Add toppings to potato.

Mexican Corn on the Cob

Ingredients:

1 ear of corn1 lime, cut into wedges
2 tablespoons Cotija cheese

2 tablespoons mayonnaise
½ garlic clove, minced
½ teaspoon chili pepper
½ teaspoon salt

Directions:

1. Mix mayo, garlic, chili pepper and salt in a small bowl.
2. Crumble up the cheese and place it in a bowl.
3. Brush the corn with the mayo-pepper mixture.
4. Wrap the corn in foil.
5. Cook for 20 to 25 minutes, or until corn is cooked.
6. Remove from foil packet and brush again with the mayo-pepper mixture.
7. Roll the corn in the Cotija cheese.
8. Enjoy.

Minty Snap Peas

Ingredients:

1 cup snap peas

1 tablespoon olive oil
3 tablespoons mint leaves, chopped
Salt, to taste

Directions:

1. Break the ends off of the snap peas.
2. Toss in a bowl with the olive oil and salt.
3. Place on foil and wrap up in a foil packet, leaving room for steam.
4. Cook for 10 to 12 minutes, or until beans start to soften.
5. Open foil packet and stir in the mint.

New Potatoes

Ingredients:

10 small new potatoes, sliced thinly

1 tablespoon olive oil
3 tablespoons water
½ teaspoon salt
½ teaspoon pepper

4 tablespoons sour cream
5 tablespoons plain yogurt
1 teaspoon chives, chopped

Directions:

1. Wash the potatoes and slice them into quarters.
2. Place the potatoes on the foil.
3. Drizzle olive oil over the potatoes.
4. Season with salt and pepper.
5. Fold up the foil packet. Leave the top open.
6. Add water to the packet and seal it, leaving room for steam.
7. Cook for 20 to 30 minutes, or until potatoes are soft.
8. Remove packet from heat and open it carefully.
9. Mix sour cream, yogurt and chives together and top potatoes with it.

Parmesan Zucchini

Ingredients:

1 large zucchini, sliced into coins

2 garlic cloves, minced
1 tablespoon butter, melted
¼ cup grated parmesan cheese
Salt and pepper, to taste.

Directions:

1. Place the zucchini on the foil.
2. Drizzle melted butter over the top of the zucchini.
3. Add the garlic and salt and pepper, to taste.
4. Wrap the foil packet up, leaving room for steam.
5. Cook for 15 to 20 minutes, or until zucchini starts to soften.
6. Open foil packet carefully and sprinkle parmesan cheese on top of zucchini.
7. Cook for an addition 2 to 3 minutes with the foil packet open.

Roasted Garlic

Ingredients:

3 cloves of garlic

2 tablespoons of olive oil
Salt and pepper, to taste

Directions:

1. Break garlic into cloves.
2. Place cloves on foil.
3. Coat cloves with olive oil.
4. Sprinkle salt and pepper on top, to taste.
5. Wrap foil packet up tightly.
6. Cook for 30 to 40 minutes, or until garlic cloves are roasted to your liking.

Rosemary Potatoes

Ingredients:

10 new potatoes, sliced thinly
½ sweet onion, sliced thinly

5 tablespoons olive oil
1 teaspoon fresh rosemary, chopped
Salt and pepper, to taste

Directions:

1. Place potatoes and onions on foil.
2. Coat with olive oil.
3. Season with rosemary, salt and pepper.
4. Wrap foil packet up tightly.
5. Cook for 20 to 25 minutes, or until potatoes are cooked to your liking. Flip the packet over after 10 minutes.
6. Remove from fire and carefully open packet.
7. Season with more salt and pepper, if necessary.

Simple Corn on the Cob

Ingredients:

1 ear of sweet corn
1 tablespoon butter
Salt and pepper, to taste

Directions:

1. Brush ear of corn liberally with butter.
2. Season with salt and pepper, to taste.
3. Wrap in foil packet.
4. Cook for 20 to 30 minutes. Turn every 5 minutes.
5. Remove foil and serve.

Simple Shrooms

Ingredients:

1 cup mushrooms, halved
½ cup salad dressing, your choice
Salt and cracked black pepper, to taste

Directions:

1. Add all ingredients to a foil packet.
2. Wrap foil packet up, leaving room for steam.
3. Cook for 15 to 20 minutes, or until mushrooms are cooked all the way through.

Summer Squash and Halibut

Ingredients:

1 halibut filet
1 summer squash, cut into coins
1 clove garlic, chopped
3 tablespoons fresh salsa
2 lime wedges

1 teaspoon oregano
½ teaspoon salt
A pinch of pepper

Directions:

1. Place fish filet on foil.
2. Place summer squash around the halibut.
3. Add garlic and fresh salsa to the top of the fish.
4. Squeeze 1 lime wedge over the fish.
5. Place the other in the packet.
6. Season with oregano, salt and pepper.
7. Wrap up foil packet tightly.
8. Cook for 12 to 15 minutes, or until fish is completely cooked.

Swiss Chard with Bacon

Ingredients:

2 cups Swiss chard
½ cup bacon bits
2 cloves garlic, minced

2 tablespoons butter
Salt and pepper, to taste

Directions:

1. Remove Swiss chard leaves from stems and place the leaves on foil.
2. Sprinkle bacon bits on top.
3. Add garlic and butter.
4. Add salt and pepper, to taste.
5. Wrap packet up, leaving room for steam.
6. Cook for 4 to 7 minutes. You want to wilt the Swiss chard leaves, but not completely cook them.

Stuffed Bell Peppers

Ingredients:

1 bell pepper, cut in half and deseeded
¼ pound ground beef or turkey
¼ onion, diced

2 tablespoons garlic powder
3 tablespoons of crushed breadcrumbs
½ teaspoon salt
½ teaspoon pepper

Directions:

1. Combine ground beef (or turkey), onion, garlic powder, breadcrumbs, salt and pepper and mix together with your hands.
2. Fill the bell pepper halves with the filling.
3. Place filled peppers face down on foil and wrap up tightly.
4. Cook for 20 to 30 minutes. Flip the packet over halfway through.
5. The peppers are done when they are soft and the meat is cooked all the way through.

Cherry Tomatoes and Feta

Ingredients:

10 to 15 cherry tomatoes
1 clove garlic, chopped
½ cup feta cheese
4 tablespoons balsamic vinegar
2 tablespoons olive oil

Directions:

1. Place tomatoes on foil.
2. Cover with feta cheese.
3. Add garlic over top of cheese.
4. Drizzle with balsamic vinegar and olive oil.
5. Wrap foil packet tightly, leaving room for steam.
6. Cook for 15 to 20 minutes, or until tomatoes are cooked to your liking.

Desserts and Assorted Dishes

This section covers desserts and recipes that didn't fall into any of the other categories, but were so tasty I didn't want to leave them out of the cookbook.

I hope you enjoy them as much as I have.

Banana Boats

Ingredients:

1 large banana

Mini marshmallows, to taste
Chocolate chips, to taste
Crumbled graham crackers, to taste

Directions:

1. Leave the banana in the peel. Slice the banana in half lengthwise.
2. Open banana up a bit and place on foil.
3. Place marshmallows and chocolate chips inside the banana.
4. Sprinkle graham cracker crumbs over the top of the marshmallows and chocolate chips.
5. Wrap the banana boat up tightly in foil.
6. Cook for 5 to 8 minutes, or until chocolate chips have melted.

Cinnamon Brown Sugar Oatmeal

Ingredients:

2 cups instant oats
½ cup water
½ cup powdered milk
3 tablespoons brown sugar
1 teaspoon cinnamon

Directions:

1. Add all ingredients to foil packet and stir together.
2. Close foil packet tightly.
3. Cook for 5 to 8 minutes, or until oatmeal is cooked.
4. Open foil packet and stir oatmeal.
5. Let sit for a couple minutes before eating. If the oatmeal is too thick, try adding a couple tablespoons of milk.

Cheesy Salsa Dip

Ingredients:

1 package Philadelphia cream cheese
1 cup Velveeta cheese
1 cup salsa
1 green onion, chopped

1 teaspoon oregano
1 teaspoon basil
1 teaspoon paprika

Directions:

1. Place cream cheese on foil.
2. Break Velveeta up and spread it over cream cheese.
3. Add oregano, basil and paprika to the top of the cheeses.
4. Wrap tightly in foil.
5. Cook for 6 to 8 minutes, or until cheese is melted.
6. Carefully open foil packet and stir cheese dip.
7. Add salsa and green onion to the top.
8. Serve with chips or crackers for dipping.

Cheesy Breadsticks

Ingredients:

Prepared pizza crust, rolled into 5 sticks
¼ cup provolone cheese, shredded

1 tablespoon parmesan cheese
½ tablespoon garlic salt
½ tablespoon olive oil

¼ cup marinara sauce

Directions:

1. Place dough on foil.
2. Brush with olive oil.
3. Season with garlic salt.
4. Sprinkle cheeses on top.
5. Wrap tightly in foil.
6. Cook for 12 to 15 minutes, or until dough is baked golden brown and cheese is melted and bubbling.
7. Serve with marinara sauce, for dipping.

Chili Cheese Fries

NOTE: This recipe can be cooked in a single packet, but it works best when cooked in two separate foil packets.

Ingredients:

½ package frozen French fries
1 cup cheddar cheese
1 can chili con carne

Salt and pepper, to taste
Cooking spray

Directions:

1. Spray the first piece of foil with cooking spray.
2. Place the fries on the foil.
3. Season the fries with salt and pepper.
4. Wrap the packet up and place it in the campfire.
5. Place the chili in the second packet.
6. Sprinkle the cheese on top.
7. Seal the packet.
8. Let both packets cook for 15 minutes, or until the French fries are cooked to your liking.
9. Open both packets and pour the chili and cheese over the fries.

Cinnamon Pineapple Doughnut Delight

Ingredients:

½ can pineapple chunks
1 plain cake doughnut

1 teaspoon butter
1 teaspoon brown sugar
1 teaspoon cinnamon
½ teaspoon olive oil

Directions:

1. Coat foil with olive oil.
2. Place pineapple chunks on the foil.
3. Break the cake doughnuts up and place them on the foil.
4. Add butter, brown sugar and cinnamon to the top.
5. Wrap foil packet up tightly.
6. Cook for 10 to 15 minutes. The recipe is complete when the butter has melted and the pineapple is heated all the way through.
7. Add a dollop of whip cream to the top to make it even better.

Easy Mac and Cheese

Ingredients:

1 cup elbow macaroni, pre-cooked
½ cup milk
1 cup Velveeta cheese, cubed
2 tablespoons butter
Salt and pepper, to taste

Directions:

1. Add all ingredients to a foil packet and stir together.
2. Seal the packet up tightly.
3. Cook the packet for 12 to 15 minutes, or until the cheese is melted.
4. Open the packet and stir the contents before serving.

Marshmallow Cinnamon Peach Halves

Ingredients:

1 peach, halved and pitted

Mini marshmallows
½ teaspoon cinnamon
1 teaspoon butter

Directions:

1. Place the peaches on the foil cut side up.
2. Place half of the butter in each half of the peach.
3. Fill the rest of the way with mini marshmallows.
4. Sprinkle cinnamon on top.
5. Close the peach so it looks whole again.
6. Wrap tightly in a foil packet.
7. Cook for 4 to 6 minutes, or until marshmallows start to melt.
8. Let cool for a few minutes before opening the packet.

Mini Fruit Pies

Ingredients:

1 mini pie crust
½ can fruit pie filling

Directions:

1. Place mini pie crust on foil.
2. Fill pie crust with pie filling.
3. Wrap pie crust tightly with foil.
4. Place in campfire. Make sure the crust stays upright, so the filling doesn't fall out.
5. Cook for 6 to 8 minutes, or until filling is hot all the way through.

Nachos

Ingredients:

1 cup tortilla chips
1 cup shredded Mexican blend cheese
½ cup refried beans

Toppings (salsa, sour cream, jalapenos, etc.)

Directions:

1. Place tortilla chips on foil.
2. Place beans on chips and spread out.
3. Spread liberal amounts on cheese onto the chips.
4. Seal foil packet tightly. Poke a few holes in the top.
5. Cook for 10 to 12 minutes, or until the cheese is melted and the beans are hot.
6. Open packet carefully and add toppings.
7. Serve hot.

Orange Caramel Cinnamon Rolls

Ingredients:

1 orange
2 cinnamon rolls

2 tablespoons of caramel

Directions:

1. Cut the orange in half.
2. Scoop out the orange, so you have two hollow shells.
3. Place one cinnamon roll in each orange half.
4. Wrap in aluminum foil and place in campfire.
5. Let cook for 10 to 15 minutes, or until cinnamon rolls start to brown.
6. Remove from fire and open foil packet.
7. Drizzle with caramel and eat while still warm.

Orange Muffins

Ingredients:

1 orange
1 package instant muffin mix

Directions:

1. Make the instant muffins following the directions on the box.
2. Cut the orange in half and scoop out the meat. Leave the peel intact. When done, you should have 2 empty orange halves.
3. Fill each of the halves with muffin mix.
4. Wrap each half in its own foil packet. Be careful to keep the orange peel upright, so the muffin mix doesn't spill out. Leave the top of the packet somewhat open in order to allow any steam that forms to escape.
5. Cook for 15 minutes, or until the muffin is cooked all the way through.

Quesadillas

Ingredients:

1 flour tortilla
½ cup shredded Mexican blend cheese

Directions:

1. Sprinkle cheese on a flour tortilla and fold it in half.
2. Place the tortilla on a piece of foil and wrap it up tightly.
3. Cook for 10 minutes. Flip the packet over after 5 minutes. Make sure cheese has melted before eating.
4. If you cook this recipe on a grill, you can get nice grill marks on your quesadilla if you leave it in one spot on the grill.

Peanut Butter S'Mores Tortillas

Ingredients:

1 flour tortilla

1 tablespoon peanut butter
Miniature marshmallows
Chocolate chips

Directions:

1. Spread peanut butter on the tortilla.
2. Add as many marshmallows and chocolate chips as you want.
3. Roll the tortilla up like a burrito.
4. Wrap it in foil.
5. Cook for 6 to 8 minutes, or until marshmallows and chocolate have melted.
6. Let cool for a few minutes, unwrap and enjoy.

Waffle Cone S'mores

Ingredients:

1 waffle cone

Miniature marshmallows
Chocolate chips
Mini pretzels
Peanut butter

Directions:

1. Fill waffle cone with marshmallows, chocolate chips, mini pretzels and peanut butter.
2. Wrap tightly in foil.
3. Place in campfire and cook for 6 to 8 minutes, or until chocolate is melted.
4. Unwrap carefully and let cool for a few minutes before eating.

The Best Recipe of All

I saved the best recipe for last. This is my family's favorite recipe because there's something in it for everyone. It doesn't matter what a person is feeling like that day, there's something in this recipe for them.

First, the ingredients:

Shrimp, peeled and deveined
Chicken, cut into cubes
Sausage, sliced diagonally
Hamburger
Steak, cubed

Baked beans
Refried beans
Pork and beans

Mushrooms, sliced
Carrots, cut into coins
Onions, diced
Red and green peppers, sliced
Baby potatoes, sliced
Green beans

Mexican blend cheese
Swiss cheese
Parmesan cheese
Cheddar cheese

Salt and pepper
BBQ sauce
Soy sauce
Ketchup
Olive oil

You're probably scratching your head right now. You're right. You can't throw all that food in a foil packet—and even if you could, it probably wouldn't taste very good. What you do is provide containers with all of that food in them and let the people in your group choose what they put in their foil packets when dinner time rolls around.

The kids love it because they get to actively participate in making dinner. They also get to make weird concoctions to try and gross each other out. The adults in your group will appreciate it because it allows them to eat whatever they want. You can cut prep time while camping down to next to nothing by cutting all of the veggies and meats ahead of time. We've done entire camping trips where this was what we did for dinner every day of the trip.

All each person in the group has to do is choose what they want in their packet, wrap it up and toss it in the fire. Cook times will vary based on the size of the packet and the food inside, but a good rule of thumb is to check the packet every 10 minutes if you aren't sure. Once you've done it a couple times, you'll know about how long each packet is going to take.

Don't forget to label the packets. Use a permanent marker to write each person's name on his or her packet. This will make life a lot easier when it comes time to unwrap and eat the packets.

Additional Reading

http://www.amazon.com/The-Family-Camping-Guide-ebook/dp/B00DVMVWF6/

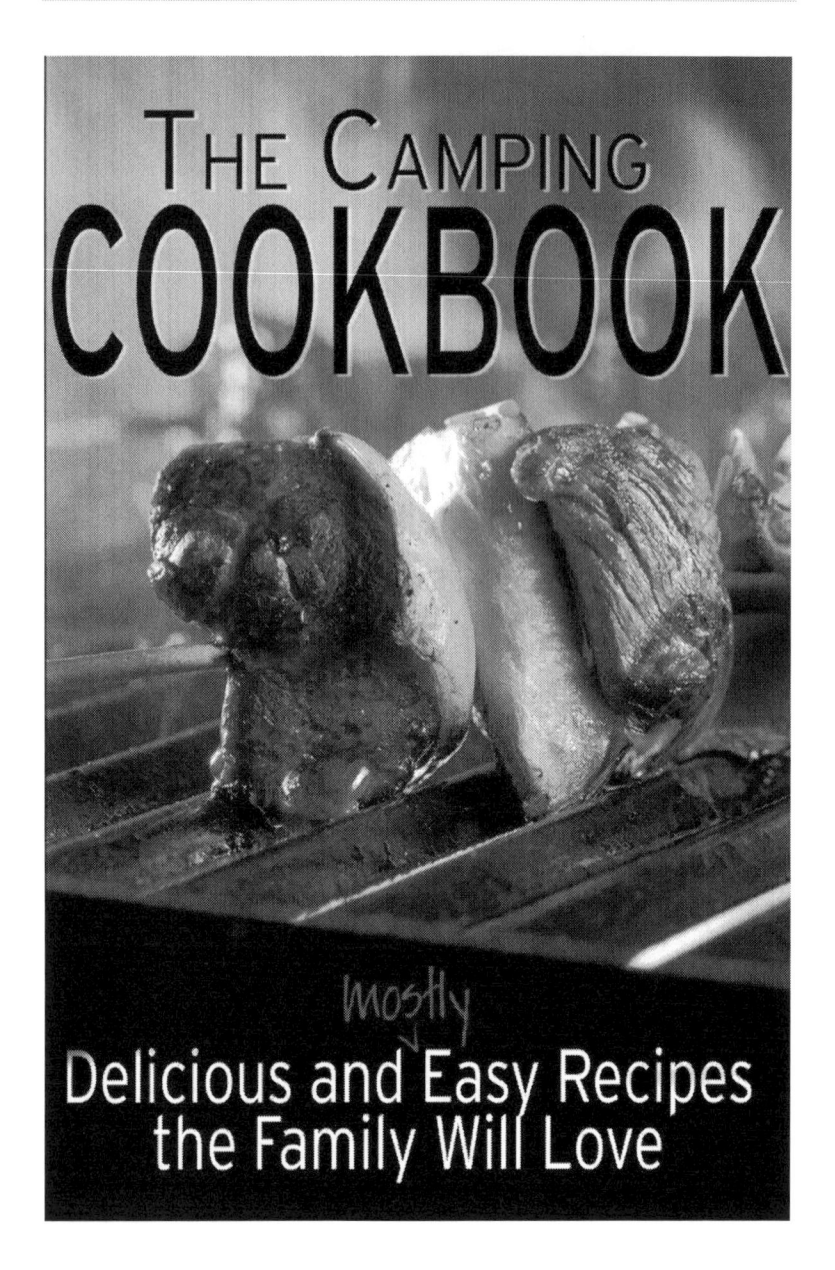

http://www.amazon.com/The-Camping-Cookbook-Delicious-ebook/dp/B00E1S8NCO/

Made in the USA
Lexington, KY
17 May 2014